GET TOGETHER with GOD MOST HOLY

GROWTH IN LOVE

Thomas M. Howell

TRILOGY
A WHOLLY OWNED SUBSIDIARY OF TBN
PROFESSIONAL PUBLISHING MEETS POWERFUL PROMOTION

GET TOGETHER WITH GOD MOST HOLY

Trilogy Christian Publishers

A Wholly Owned Subsidiary of Trinity Broadcasting Network

2442 Michelle Drive, Tustin, CA 92780

Copyright © 2024 by Thomas M. Howell

Scripture quotations marked MSG are taken from *THE MESSAGE*, copyright (c) 1993, 2002, 2018 by Eugene H. Peterson. Used by permission of NavPress. All rights reserved. Represented by Tyndale House Publishers, Inc.

Scripture quotations marked NIV are taken from the Holy Bible, New International Version®, NIV®. Copyright © 1973, 1978, 1984, 2011 by Biblica, Inc.™ Used by permission of Zondervan. All rights reserved worldwide. www.zondervan.com. The "NIV" and "New International Version" are trademarks registered in the United States Patent and Trademark Office by Biblica, Inc.™

All rights reserved, including the right to reproduce this book or portions thereof in any form whatsoever.

For information, address Trilogy Christian Publishing

Rights Department, 2442 Michelle Drive, Tustin, CA 92780.

Trilogy Christian Publishing/ TBN and colophon are trademarks of Trinity Broadcasting Network.

For information about special discounts for bulk purchases, please contact Trilogy Christian Publishing.

Trilogy Disclaimer: The views and content expressed in this book are those of the author and may not necessarily reflect the views and doctrine of Trilogy Christian Publishing or the Trinity Broadcasting Network.

10 9 8 7 6 5 4 3 2 1

Library of Congress Cataloging-in-Publication Data is available.

ISBN 979-8-89597-214-4

ISBN (ebook) 979-8-89597-215-1

THIS BOOK IS DEDICATED TO:

The memory of my brother, Will Howell, who lived his life well, showing his love to God, his family and friends. He was an outstanding teacher and author. He was a great encouragement to me.

To Claudia Christian, a fine actor, author, and founder and CEO of the nonprofit *Options Save Lives*, formally *C Three Foundation*. She has inspired me through her words and life. She shows her faith in God through her actions. Claudia gave me the inspiration to write this book.

KEY PASSAGE

Teacher, which is the greatest commandment in the Law? Jesus replied: "Love the Lord your God with all your heart and with all your soul and with all your mind." This is the first greatest commandment. And the second is like it: "Love your neighbor as yourself." All the Law and the Prophets hang on these two commandments.

Matthew 22:36-40 NIV

INTRODUCTION

Get Together with God Most Holy is a weekly devotional designed to guide you through growing your faith in God, and helping you to gain a deeper relationship with Him. It will also help deepen relationships with your family, friends, and neighbors. Part one is twenty-six weeks on loving God, and Part two is twenty-six weeks on loving others.

The key passage (Matthew 22:36-40) provides us with the theme of this devotional: to experience growth in love to be able to truly and fully love God; then be able to love others as we love ourselves. This is how the passage reads in The Message Bible.

Jesus said, "Love the Lord your God with all your passion and prayer and intelligence." This is the most important, the first on any list. But there is a second to set alongside it: "Love others as well as you love yourself." These two commands are pegs; everything in God's Law and the Prophets hangs from them.

Matthew 22:36-40 MSG

The Greek word used for love in this passage is the verb form of unconditional love. It is an active love flowing through us, a love that moves our hearts. The success of living according God's Word is dependent on these two commands.

It is my hope that this devotional will be an instrument enabling you to enjoy spending time with God, and that it will also help deepen your relationship with Him and your family, friends, and neighbors. May you be greatly blessed as you spend time with God and see how much He loves you.

PART ONE
LOVING GOD

WEEK ONE

For God so loved the world that he gave his only Son, that whoever believes in him shall not perish but have eternal life. For God did not send his Son into the world to condemn the world, but to save the world through him. Whoever believes in him is not condemned, but whoever does not believe stands condemned already because he has not believed in the name of God's one and only Son.

John 3:16-18 NIV

The first step to loving God is understanding how He first loved us and saved us through Jesus, His Son. Imagine, if you will, God's great love for all people, created in His image, that He would send His Son Jesus to redeem all who choose to put their faith in Him. Imagine a grace given to all who believe and at the same time given to each believer individually; a love for all and at the same time, a love for you personally.

THOUGHTS TO PONDER THIS WEEK

- » Consider the significance that God created humans, males and females, in His own image. (Genesis 1:27)
- » Reflect on God's deep love for you. (Romans 8:38-39)
- » Have confidence through your faith that you are no longer condemned. (Romans 8:1-2)

No matter what we have done, how many times we stumble and fall, or how unworthy we feel, God the Father loves us. In fact His love is so deep that He sent His Son Jesus to redeem us by dying a humble death on a cross. Then He rose from the grave three days later, proving His power over death and that all who trust in Him will have eternal life.

My Notes

WEEK TWO

"God demonstrates his own love for us in this: While we were still sinners, Christ died for us."

Romans 5:8 NIV

Even though I was a sinner away from God, He demonstrated His unconditional love for me by restoring my relationship with Him through the death of Jesus Christ. What an amazing love our Holy God has for us. We turned away from Him for the ways of the world and had no way to turn back to Him. Because of His love for us, He restored our relationship with Him though Jesus.

Thoughts to Ponder This Week

» Reflect on the saving grace of Jesus, who shows mercy and patience towards us. He is trustworthy, deserving of our full acceptance. (1 Timothy 1:15-16)
» Ponder how Jesus, the righteous, suffered for us, the unrighteous, so we might be saved. (1 Peter 3:18)
» God's love is perfect; our love is imperfect.

How marvelous is the love of God that He would unconditionally love me while I was still unworthy of such a love. Through His deep love for us, God shows us how we ought to love. While our love for God grows deeper, through the Holy Spirit He demonstrates how we are to love others.

My Notes

WEEK THREE

"This is how God showed his love among us: He sent his one and only Son into the world that we might live through him."

1 John 4:9 NIV

God's amazing love toward the unloving is proven through the sacrifice of Jesus so that we may enjoy eternal life with God the Father, God the Son, and God the Holy Spirit, Three in One. Being in a loving relationship with God gives us purpose to live by. Since God loves us, we should love Him in return and love each other as well.

Thoughts to Ponder This Week

» Jesus is the only way that God's perfect justice and perfect love could both be satisfied.
» Has there ever been a time in your life that you felt so alone, so unworthy, that you didn't deserve unconditional love?
» Know that God loves you and wants a relationship with you, one that will bring incredible peace into your life, even in the hard times.

A good friend of mine went through some tremendous hardships in her life. She struggled with something that she called her monster. This monster had control over her life. She did battle with it for years. My friend felt alone and unworthy. She was living a life in total hopelessness; even to the point of considering killing herself. The monster had a heart of wickedness and it was destroying my friend's life, slowly killing her in the process. My friend started to pray hard but didn't feel God heard her. She didn't think He loved her or that she was even worthy of His love. She finally won the battle with her monster and is grateful to God for saving her life and giving her the desire to help others who are struggling. She has helped many people, saving their lives. God loved her even when she thought He didn't. Believe it or not, God loves you and wants to be in your life.

My Notes

WEEK FOUR

"I have hidden your word in my heart that I might not sin against you. Praise be to you, O Lord; teach me your decrees."

Psalm 119:11-12 NIV

Sadly there are people out there that use the Bible as a weapon to bring judgment on others and lift themselves up as being better than anyone else. However, that is not what the psalmist is displaying here. He is saying how he loves God's Word and how precious it is to him. The reason he finds it to be valued is because of his love for God; he does not want to sin against God but rather live in a way that pleases God. Then he prays to God, giving Him praise out of his love for God and then asks for wisdom to understand God's Word.

Thoughts to Ponder This Week

» There is a difference between studying the Bible and meditating on its words. Both have their purpose.
» Do you ask for the Holy Spirit to give you understanding of the Word?
» Loving the Bible is a form of loving God in that it helps build our relationship with God.

I enjoy studying the Bible when I am putting together a lesson or a message, and yes, writing this book. However, I also need to spend time just reading the Bible and praying. I would like to encourage you to spend some time each day reading the Bible and talking with God. If you miss a day or more, don't get upset with yourself. Remember, it's not meant to be a sacrament you have to follow but rather a time to build your relationship with God.

My Notes

WEEK FIVE

"If you love me, you will obey what I command. And I will ask the Father, and he will give you another Counselor to be with you forever—the Spirit of truth. The world cannot accept him, because it neither sees him nor knows him. But you know him, for he lives with you and will be in you."

John 14:15-17 NIV

Our obedience to Jesus is an outpouring of our love for Him. For us who put our faith in Jesus, we have the Spirit of truth (Holy Spirit) who lives with us and in us. He guides us and helps us grow. The unbeliever does not have the Holy Spirit nor do they know Him.

Thoughts to Ponder This Week

- » Legalism is a ritualistic obedience.
- » Obedience as an outpouring of love builds a relationship.
- » A life spent loving God leads to good relationships.

When I was in high school, I would be in church on Sunday, firmly believing I would do better living the Christian life. The next day, I would be at school telling dirty jokes, using horrible words, and being rude, none of which showed Christian love. This went on for a long time until one Sunday night in church it came to me. I could not solve this problem on my own; I needed to start depending on God and listening to the Holy Spirit. That started bringing a change in my life. It is not enough to know the Bible; we need to listen to the Holy Spirit as well. When you spend time with God reading the Bible and listening to the Spirit of truth, you will be able to fight off temptation better than when you are not spending time with God.

My Notes

WEEK SIX

"If anyone loves me, he will obey my teaching. My Father will love him, and we will come to him and make our home with him. He who does not love me will not obey my teaching. These words you hear are not my own; they belong to the Father who sent me."

John 14:23-24 NIV

We should not follow God's Word as a ritualistic act of religion, which is of no benefit to us. Following God's Word should be the result of our love for Him. Our life with God isn't about religion; it's about a loving relationship, a relationship where God loves us and we love Him.

Thoughts to Ponder This Week

- » The Bible is a guide to a better relationship for those who believe in and love God.
- » Remember, salvation is a one-time act in the life of the believer through Jesus Christ.
- » After that, the believer spends the rest of his/her life growing in a deeper relationship with God.

Remember, reading the Bible and going to church as an act of religion holds no meaning to God. What God desires is our reading the Bible and following it as an outpouring of our love for Him. He wants our deeds and worship to come from our hearts through a loving, growing relationship with the Almighty.

My Notes

WEEK SEVEN

"All authority in heaven and on earth has been given to me. Therefore go and make disciples of all nations, baptizing them in the name of the Father and of the Son and of the Holy Spirit, and teaching them to obey everything I have commanded you. And surely I am with you always, to the very end of the age."

Matthew 28:18-20 NIV

Here in the great commission ,we see three ways that we can show our love for God. We will look at the first one this week: making disciples throughout the world. We have discussed how those who love God obey God. Here Jesus states all authority has been given to Him and He gives us the great commission. When you consider the time and energy it takes to build a relationship with someone and then discipling them, you must wonder if this passage should be in part two of this book. Well, it is here to help you realize how taking the message that God loves them to people and discipling them is indeed a way of showing your love for God.

Thoughts to Ponder This Week

- » Reflect on how the same action can be an expression of both loving God and loving your neighbor.
- » Having a heart to disciple requires first, a love of God and second a love for others.
- » Discipling someone is helping them grow in their relationship with God.

Showing compassion for those who need to know how much God loves them is an outpouring of your love for God. As your love for God grows deeper, so will your compassion for others. The deeper a relationship you have with God, the deeper a relationship you can have with others.

My Notes

WEEK EIGHT

"All authority in heaven and on earth has been given to me. Therefore go and make disciples of all nations, baptizing them in the name of the Father and of the Son and of the Holy Spirit, and teaching them to obey everything I have commanded you. And surely I am with you always, to the very end of the age."

Matthew 28:18-20 NIV

When a discipling relationship leads a person to faith in Jesus, we are told to baptize them. This is not a requirement for salvation, but rather a symbol of their old life being replaced by a renewed life in Jesus. It marks the start of a loving relationship with God.

Thoughts to Ponder This Week

» How you are baptized (by sprinkling or by immersion) isn't as important as what it symbolizes.
» A life separated from God is being restored to a true relationship with Him.
» A life is restored by God's love according to the will of the Father, through the grace of the Son, and guided by the Holy Spirit.

Sometimes I get so wrapped up in the affairs of the world that I neglect my relationship with God. As with any relationship, we need to spend time nurturing our relationship with God to keep it healthy. Galatians 5:25 NIV is one of my verses for guiding my life. "Since we live by the Spirit, let us keep in step with the Spirit."

My Notes

WEEK NINE

"All authority in heaven and on earth has been given to me. Therefore go and make disciples of all nations, baptizing them in the name of the Father and of the Son and of the Holy Spirit, and teaching them to obey everything I have commanded you. And surely I am with you always, to the very end of the age."

Matthew 28:18-20 NIV

Here we are told to teach the new believer to obey all of God's commands. This does not mean to teach them to legalistically follow God's rule book; rather, it means to teach them to obey God out of their love for Him. Remember, the greatest commandment is to fully love God, and the second is to love those around you. It is these two that everything else is dependent on.

Thoughts to Ponder This Week

- » Our goal should be to perform our training in love. (1 Timothy 1:5)
- » We should have a sincere faith. (1 Timothy 1:5)
- » This can only be done through a loving relationship with God.

Normally we think of discipleship as being one person teaching another person. However, it can also be two believers guiding each other or a small group encouraging each other. Remember, guiding someone in their faith can only be done by a believer who truly loves God and has compassion for others.

My Notes

WEEK TEN

Read Luke 7:36-47

Then he turned toward the woman and said to Simon, "Do you see this woman? I came into your house. You did not give me any water for my feet, but she wet my feet with her tears and wiped them with her hair. You did not give me a kiss, but this woman from the time I enter, has not stopped kissing my feet. You did not put oil on my head, but she has poured perfume on my feet. Therefore, I tell you, her many sins have been forgiven, for she loved much. But he who has been forgiven little loves little."

Luke 7:44-47 NIV

Picture if you will: when a woman, who was considered unworthy to be with "the honorable people," hears Jesus is at a dinner at a Pharisee's house she goes there to see Jesus. As she cries, she shows her love toward Jesus with a humble heart. She wipes away the tears that fell on the feet of Jesus with her hair. Then she kissed them and poured perfume on them. Compare that with the host who didn't give Jesus water for his feet, greet him with a kiss, or pour oil on his head; all things a host would be expected to do for his guest. Jesus responded to this humble act of love by saying that her sins have been forgiven, for she had shown great love toward Him.

Thoughts to Ponder This Week

» Are you aware of God's grace in your life?
» Are you aware you are a sinner and have been forgiven?
» Are you aware that God loves you and considers you to be holy, without sin?

Those of us who love God with a humble heart and put our faith in Jesus have the grace of God in our lives. Even though unworthy, we have been forgiven and made worthy through Jesus Christ. The worthy paid the price for the unworthy that we might live.

My Notes

WEEK ELEVEN

Read John 20:10-18

"...but Mary stood outside the tomb crying. As she wept, she bent over to look into the tomb and saw two angels in white, seated where Jesus' body had been, one at the head and the other at the foot."

John 20:11-12 NIV

Mary loved Jesus and now felt a great loss. He was dead, and she did not know He rose from the grave. As far she was concerned, He was crucified and she would not see Him again. She felt a great loss that broke her heart. Now His body was gone and her heart ached with sorrow. Imagine the joy Mary felt when she saw Jesus was indeed alive, the feelings rushing through her soul. "How can this be; He was dead, I saw it and yet now He is alive. What a wonderful miracle, Jesus is alive."

Thoughts to Ponder This Week

» Reflect on the joy felt at the birth of Jesus, Immanuel, God with us.
» Consider the anguish and sense of loss at the death of Jesus on the cross.
» Think about the hope and joy that comes with the words "He's alive; He's alive indeed."

God wants our love. He desires a healthy relationship with us. This requires spending time with God, as with any relationship. Often when we are so full of activity that we aren't spending quality time reading our Bible, praying, or worshiping, we start to feel God isn't there. We start to feel a loss of faith and hope. We begin to feel that God no longer loves us, and we may even feel unworthy of His love. Know that none of this is true. God is still there, wanting our hearts. He loves us and wants to bring joy into our lives. God loves you more than you know.

My Notes

WEEK TWELVE

Read John 21:15-17

"And he has given us this command: Whoever loves God must also love his brother."

1 John 4:21 NIV

Three times Jesus asks Peter, "Do you love me?" Three times Peter says, "I love You." Three times Jesus says, "Then take care of My sheep." Our love of Jesus ought to bring the response of love and compassion for others.

Thoughts to Ponder This Week

- » Do you wholly love God?
- » Do you love God unconditionally?
- » If the answer is yes (and I hope it is) then you will show love and compassion towards others as a natural outcome of your love of God.

Peter was not perfect, but he loved Jesus; and Jesus was patient as He taught Peter to be the leader He desired him to be. I am far from perfect; however, I love God, and He is tremendously patient with me as He guides me with love. If you love God, know that even though you are not perfect, He loves you and will guide with patience. God has different amazing plans for each of us, but we are all called to show love and compassion to each other through our love of God.

My Notes

WEEK THIRTEEN

Read Acts 21:7-14

When we heard this, we and the people there pleaded with Paul not to go up to Jerusalem. Then Paul answered, "Why are you weeping and breaking my heart? I am ready not only to be bound, but also to die in Jerusalem for the name of the Lord Jesus. When he would not be dissuaded, we gave up and said, "The Lord's will be done."

Acts 21:12-14 NIV

Agabus, a prophet, gave a message from the Holy Spirit that the Jewish leaders in Jerusalem would bind Paul and turn him over to the Roman authorities. Here we have two reactions to this prophecy. First, the Christians there with Paul took the prophecy as a warning and urged Paul not to go to Jerusalem. Paul saw it as what was meant to be, and said he was not only ready to be bound, but also to die for Jesus.

Thoughts to Ponder This Week

- » Consider Paul's love of God.
- » Consider how Paul devoted his life to following God's will.
- » Paul's love and devotion was such that he was willing to die for Jesus.

Paul was an upright man, a leader among the Jews. He was a Pharisee of the Pharisees, and a religious follower of the law. He was considered a good man among the people, but all that was worthless for his salvation. Paul was not saved by his works, but rather by coming to faith in Jesus. It was by that faith that Paul learned the difference of living by the law and living by grace. Paul was then able to fully love God. May our love of God grow so that we may bring glory to Him and be able to show compassion to others, loving them as we love ourselves. Remember, it is okay to love ourselves.

My Notes

WEEK FOURTEEN

"Peace to the brothers, and love with faith from God the Father and the Lord Jesus Christ. Grace to all who love our Lord Jesus Christ with an undying love."

Ephesians 6:23-24 NIV

Paul closes his letter to the believers in Ephesus with a prayer or benediction. Here we see the close relationship between God and those who truly love Him and put their trust in the grace of Jesus Christ. Faith and love work hand in hand to open our hearts to God. Paul desires for the readers of this letter to have an undying love for Jesus.

Thoughts to Ponder This Week

- » Remember, it was God who first loved us and drew us to Him by the Holy Spirit.
- » Remember, all you need to do to be saved is confess with your mouth and believe in your heart (Romans 10:9).
- » Remember, we show our love for God by following His will for our lives (Romans 12:2).

A person who truly believes in Jesus no longer lives by the pattern of their old life; but rather shows their love to God by living according to His perfect will. This is done by the renewing of our minds through the Holy Spirit. This is a lifelong process of building a close relationship with God. It is much like how two people spend their lives together building a close relationship that continually leads to a deeper love for each other.

My Notes

WEEK FIFTEEN

"Though you have not seen him, you love him; and even though you do not see him now, you believe in him and are filled with an inexpressible and glorious joy, for you are receiving the goal of your faith, the salvation of your souls."

> 1 Peter 1:8-9 NIV

"Thomas said to him, 'My Lord and my God!' Then Jesus told him, Because you have seen me. You have believed; Blessed are those who have not seen and yet have believed.'"

> John 20:28-29 NIV

Thoughts to Ponder This Week

- » God loves us and calls by the will of the Father,
- » By the grace of Jesus the Son,
- » And by the calling of the Holy Spirit.

When the disciples told Thomas that Jesus was alive and had visited them, he said he would not believe Jesus was alive unless he saw Him. It is worth noting here that Thomas was not asking for anything more than what the other disciples saw. When Jesus came again and Thomas saw Him, he was overcome with joy and believed what his eyes saw. Jesus said, in effect, you believed having seen me; however, those who believe without seeing are blessed. Indeed, we who believe and love Jesus, not seeing, are blessed. We receive great joy because we are saved; however, we do not feel that joy all the time nor do we feel love for God all the time. Remember, we cannot trust in feelings alone. When I made the choice to love God, I made it to love regardless of feelings that come and go. Remember, God chose to love us as we were, and because of that love we are able to love Him and have that love grow.

My Notes

WEEK SIXTEEN

"God is not unjust; he will not forget your work and the love you have shown him as you have helped his people and continue to help them."

Hebrews 6:10 NIV

We show our faith in and love for God through our compassion for others as we help them with their needs. God remembers our service and love we have for Him. We see here how love for God and love for others go hand in hand.

Thoughts to Ponder This Week

- » Do you love God?
- » Do you have compassion for others?
- » Do you see how the two together make the world a better place?

Our love for God is intended to be more than a noun, a thing, or an object; it is intended also to be a verb, action, or act toward God and others. If a way to show our love to God is by showing compassion to others, who then are the others? Are they not anyone who comes across our path in need, regardless of their ethnic, social, or economic background? Whether they are likeable or not is not the concern, but rather their need for someone to care for them.

My Notes

WEEK SEVENTEEN

"We love because he first loved us. If anyone says, 'I love God,' yet hates his brother, he is a liar. For anyone who does not love his brother, whom he has seen, cannot love God, whom he has not seen. And he has given us this command: Whoever loves God must also love His brother."

1 John 4:19-21 NIV

In this passage loving or hating one's brother refers to the relationship between believers, brothers and sisters in the Lord, if you will. Here John calls out those who claim to love God and yet hate their fellow believer as being a liar. Not loving a brother or sister is an example that the person may confess his or her love for God but they do not believe in their heart (Romans 10:9).

Thoughts to Ponder This Week

» You are fully saved through Jesus once and for all.
» Becoming more loving and compassionate is a lifelong process.
» Loving our brother or sister is an outpouring of our love for God.

There are those who are not easy for us to love or even have compassion for. In fact they can bring out anger in us against them. However, we are called to have compassion for them, to love them as our brother or sister in Jesus Christ. When I was in grade school, there was a neighbor boy who went out of his way to bully me, and I didn't like him even after I grew up. Just thinking of his name brought out anger in me. One day years ago, we ran, into each other and he remembered me and asked if I was Tom Howell. I said yes. He said his name (which brought out feelings of anger in me) and said he was sorry for the way he treated me and asked my forgiveness. With those words the anger was gone and I could honestly forgive him. He had become a Christian and thought about how he treated me for years. In that moment when we ran into each other, God healed both his guilt and my anger and we could love each other as fellow believers. I don't know where he is now, but I thank God for that encounter.

My Notes

WEEK EIGHTEEN

"Let love and faithfulness never leave you; bind them around your neck, write them on the tablet of your heart. Then you will win favor and a good name in the sight of God and man. Trust in the Lord with all your heart and lean not on your own understanding; in all your ways acknowledge him, and he will make your paths straight."

Proverbs 3:3-6 NIV

Thoughts to Ponder This Week

- » Love God: Strong affection towards Him, devoted to Him, worships Him.
- » Faithful to God: loyal to Him and His Word, dependable, dedicated, and reliable.
- » Trust God: Place your confidence in Him, to have assurance He loves and cares for you.

Love, faithfulness, and trust: three concepts that work together in one's relationship with God. In these verses, we are encouraged to love God and to be faithful to Him. We are told that if we don't lean on our own understanding, but rather acknowledge and trust God in all that we do, He will guide us in the way we should go. How often do we follow the way of the world instead of God? The key is, like with any healthy relationship, we need to spend time building it so we can become closer to God.

My Notes

WEEK NINETEEN

"I love you, O Lord, my strength. The Lord is my rock, my fortress and my deliverer; my God is my rock, in whom I take refuge. He is my shield and the horn of my salvation, my stronghold. I call to the Lord, who is worthy of praise, and I am saved from my enemies."

Psalm 18:1-3 NIV

This is a psalm of King David, servant of God. Here David expresses his love for God, and his gratefulness and praise for God saving him from his enemies. Perhaps this is a song David sings whenever God delivers him from his enemies or when he wishes to remember those times. One thing for sure is that through these words David honors God and shows his great love and gratefulness towards the most holy God.

Thoughts to Ponder This Week

» In these words David describes a great God, yet God is far greater than David's description.
» God is far greater than any words we can come up with to describe Him.
» I am thankful that God is bigger and more majestic than I can possibly describe; how about you?

How majestic and wonderful is God whom we love? No words or thoughts can possibly hope to come close to describing His greatness; yet God gives us enough understanding to realize His love for us and to be able to love Him in return. As our relationship with God grows deeper, we begin to know Him more. How wonderful it is that God our creator desires a relationship with us and we are part of His family through the blood of Jesus.

My Notes

WEEK TWENTY

(Read Psalm 31:1-8 and Psalm 31:21-22)

"Love the Lord, all his saints! The Lord preserves the faithful, but the proud he pays back in full. Be strong and take heart, all you who hope in the Lord."

Psalm 31:23-24 NIV

Psalm 31 is another psalm of David in which he praises God for his protection from his enemies. In these last two verses, he calls the faithful to love the Lord who cares for them. They are to remain strong in their hope for God will not disappoint. Even when all seems hopeless, they can rely on the merciful God who will carry them though.

THOUGHTS TO PONDER THIS WEEK

» God is great and mighty.
» Who can come against God?
» God saves those who love Him.

There are times in my life when I am going through a challenging struggle and I feel despair rather than hope. It is in those times that I must choose to put my trust in God, my strong hold and salvation, and keep hope alive. Regardless of our feelings, we can know that God loves those who believe in Him and will carry us to victory. Glory to God, the rock of my salvation.

My Notes

WEEK TWENTY-ONE

"As the deer pants for streams of water, so my soul pants for you, O God. My soul thirsts for God, for the living God. When can I go and meet with God?"

Psalm 42:1-2 NIV

Even though it doesn't say so, the style of Psalm 42 would indicate it was written by David. One thing for sure is that it was written by someone who loved God and at the time he wrote it he was going through some challenges and didn't feel God's presence. In these first two verses, the author draw a wonderful picture of his love for God. Just like a deer thirsts for water and even needs it, so does the author desire the presence of God in his life and even needs it.

Thoughts to Ponder This Week

» For you, is going to church a religious act or an act of worship?
» Our relationship with God should have a positive effect on our relationship with others.
» Does your soul thirst for a vital relationship with God?

There are times in my life that I feel God's love and the joy He brings. My soul is warmed by His presence. Then there are other times when I don't feel His presence and I long to feel it again. It's like someone you have a special relationship with. When you are together all is well, and when you are apart you long to be with them again. They are all you can think about. The difference is that with God, He is always present. When we don't feel that God is there, we need to trust that He is and He loves us.

My Notes

WEEK TWENTY-TWO

"I love the Lord, for he heard my voice; he heard my cry for mercy. Because he turned his ear to me I will call on him as long as I live."

(Psalm 116:1-2 NIV)

Here the author says he loves God because He heard his prayer for mercy. God heard and answered, and as a result the author will call on God with devotion the rest of his life.

Thoughts to Ponder This Week

» God hears and answers our prayers.
» Do you love God with a heart of devotion?
» Will you devote the rest of your life to God?

Have you ever thought about how amazing it is that God Almighty, creator of everything, hears our prayers from on high? Not only that, He answers them in ways that are beyond our understanding. I find it amazing that God reaches out across all of creation to me and cares about my concerns. He truly deserves my love and devotion for the rest of my life and beyond. May you call upon the Lord with confidence because of His love for you and yours in return.

My Notes

WEEK TWENTY-THREE

"Great peace have they who love your law, and nothing can make them stumble. I wait for your salvation, O Lord, and I follow your commands."

Psalm 119:165-166 NIV

Note here it does not say great peace to those who follow the law perfectly. No one can do that. Nor does it say salvation comes from following the law. Our salvation comes only from God through Jesus Christ. However, loving and knowing the Word does help keep us out of trouble.

Thoughts to Ponder This Week

- » Knowing the Bible is only the first part; we need to live according to what we learn.
- » It does not do any good to act on the Word in a legalistic manner; it didn't work for the Pharisee and it will not work for us.
- » It is only through our love of God and His Word that our actions will have any meaning.

Our hope is not based on how well we follow God's law but rather based on God's love, mercy, and grace through our Lord Jesus Christ. That being said, the deeper our relationship with God grows, the more we will want to follow His will out of our love of Him.

Now as we move on to the last three weeks of part one, "Loving God," we will have a discussion about showing our love for God through praise and worship. After all, who is more worthy to receive praise and worship than God Almighty?

My Notes

WEEK TWENTY-FOUR

"I will exalt you, my God the King: I will praise your name forever and ever. Every day I will praise you and extol your name forever and ever. Great is the Lord and most worthy of praise; his greatness no one can fathom."

Psalm 145:1-3 NIV

In this Psalm of David, we see his great love and adoration towards God. David proclaims that God is the King and is highly worthy of praise, that God is so great no one can comprehend His greatness. It is within the heart of David to worship God every day forever.

Thoughts to Ponder This Week

» Do you praise God every day?
» Do you have the desire to worship God forever?
» Any concept we can come up with of God would be too small.

I am thankful that any perception I could have of God would be too small, because any god I could perceive would be too small. I am deeply grateful that God is beyond our understanding, and yet He makes Himself known to us. God is truly worthy of our adoration. Should we not long to worship him through our praise and deeds, to be thankful for His love and love Him the rest of our lives?

My Notes

WEEK TWENTY-FIVE

"Praise the Lord. How good it is to sing praises to our God, how pleasant and fitting to praise him! Sing to the Lord with thanksgiving; make music to our God on the harp."

Psalm 147:1, 7 NIV

God is worthy of our worship and love, is He not? After all, He loved us first and paved the way to our salvation. It is defiantly fitting that we should sing praise to our Lord with all our hearts, and it should be pleasant as well. I am grateful for what God has done in my life and what He is doing.

Thoughts to Ponder This Week

- » Is your worship of God empty worship, or is it honest worship from your heart?
- » God desires our true worship and admiration.
- » True worship is an act of our love.

Note here that empty worship is not the same as worshiping without feeling. Empty worship can be filled with emotion or it can simply be a religious act. True worship, on the other hand, can be filled with joy and passion or be a challenge to do when you do not feel like it. Whatever the case, true worship comes from the heart through our love of God. We can worship God as individuals or together with our brothers and sisters in the Lord. In week twenty-six, we will be looking at showing our love of God through worshiping Him with our Christian family as well as in our personal time with God.

My Notes

WEEK TWENTY-SIX

Praise the Lord. Praise God in his sanctuary; praise him in his mighty heavens. Praise him for his acts of power; praise him for his surpassing greatness. Praise him with the sounding of the trumpet, praise him with the harp and lyre, praise him with tambourine and dancing, praise him with the strings and flute, praise him with the clash of cymbals, praise him with resounding cymbals. Let everything that has breath praise the Lord. Praise the Lord.

Psalm 150 NIV

Psalm 150 is my favorite psalm and one of my favorite passages in the whole Bible. It is a great example of worshiping God out of our love for Him. First off, we are called to worship God with our church family. He is worthy of our praise because of His mighty power and greatness, along with His compassionate love for us. There is a sizeable list here of ways to praise God, but not an exclusive list. Bottom line here is that when we come together to worship our Lord we should be willing to use all our gifts and talents He has given us. At this point, remember we are not called to be the best in our worship, but rather to give our best to God through our worship.

THOUGHTS TO PONDER THIS WEEK

- » Do you love God with all your heart?
- » Do you worship God with all that you have?
- » Do you enjoy spending time with God?

When I spend time with God I like to have my Bible and guitar with me. I will read, sing songs, and pray (talk with God). It is like my own little worship time to spend alone with God. Talking with my brother Will, we found out that we both spent time with God that way. I tell the story not to imply that you should spend time with God like that, but rather to encourage you to discover your own special way to spend time alone with God.

My Notes

KEY PASSAGE

"Teacher, which is the greatest commandment in the Law?" Jesus replied: "Love the Lord your God with all your heart and with all your soul and with all your mind." This is the first greatest commandment. And the second is like it: "Love your neighbor as yourself." All the Law and the Prophets hang on these two commandments.

Matthew 22:36-40 NIV

Jesus said, "Love the Lord your God with all your passion and prayer and intelligence." This is the most important, the first on any list. But there is a second to set alongside it: "Love others as well as you love yourself." These two commands are pegs; everything in God's Law and the Prophets hangs from them.

Matthew 22:36-40 MSG

PART TWO
LOVING OTHERS

WEEK TWENTY-SEVEN

"'Love the Lord your God with all your heart and with all your soul and with all your mind.' This is the first greatest commandment. And the second is like it: 'Love your neighbor as yourself.'"

Matthew 22:37-39 NIV

"Love others as well as you love yourself."

Matthew 22:39b MMG

There are two things needed for us to truly love others unconditionally. First off, we need to love God and let His love flow through us to others. Second, in order to love others we must love ourselves.

Thoughts to Ponder This Week

» Do you love God with all you heart, soul, and mind?
» Do you love yourself unconditionally?
» Do you love others with a compassionate heart?

When we talk about this passage, there is a lot said about loving God and loving others; however, there is little said, if anything, about loving ourselves. It is almost as if that part of the passage isn't even there. However, loving ourselves is an important part of being able to love others. If we truly love ourselves unconditionally, we will be able to truly love others unconditionally. Here are some reasons you should honor God by loving yourself. First off, you were created by God in His image (Genesis 1:26-27). Second: as a way of thanking God for wonderfully creating you (Psalm139:14). Thirdly: God loves you and desires a personal relationship with you (John 3:16-18). By the way, these are also reasons you should love others.

My Notes

WEEK TWENTY-EIGHT

"If I speak in the tongues of men and angels, but have not love, I am only a resounding gong or a clanging cymbal. If I have the gift of prophecy and can fathom all mysteries and all knowledge, and if I have a faith that can move mountains, but have not love, I am nothing. If I give all I possess to the poor and surrender my body to the flames, but have not love, I gain nothing."

                    1 Corinthians. 13:1-3 NIV

We can have great talent and do many good deeds, but if we do them without love they are just for show. They hold no real meaning as if being nothing. In reality, without love we gain nothing from them.

Thoughts to Ponder This Week

- » Do you do good deeds for others?
- » Do you do good deeds for your own profit?
- » Are they acts of love?

Many good deeds are done simply for show without unconditional love. They may also be done as a means to self-gain or self-gratification. No matter how talented someone is or how much they give, if their good acts are done without unconditional love they will gain nothing. The goal for the believer is to let the unconditional love of God flow through our hearts towards others, showing them kindness. It is how we can truly show God's image through our lives. The deeper our relationship with God grows, the more we are capable of unconditional love towards others.

My Notes

WEEK TWENTY-NINE

"Love is patient, love is kind. It does not envy, it does not boast, it is not proud. It is not rude, it is not self-seeking, it is not easily angered, it keeps no record of wrongs. Love does not delight in evil but rejoices with the truth. It always protects, always ways trusts, always hopes, always perseveres."

1 Corinthians 13:4-7 NIV

Here Paul defines unconditional love, what it is and what it isn't. It is quite a list, and the kind of love God expects us to show towards others. Has God flipped out, you are thinking. Does He really want us to do the impossible?

Thoughts to Ponder This Week

» Unconditional love is what we are called to give to others.
» Is it even possible to love others in such a way?
» How can it be possible for us to love unconditionally?

It is possible and God has not flipped out. However, it is not possible by our own power or will. It is only possible by the Holy Spirit flowing through us, guiding us and allowing God's love to flow through our hearts. It is through belief in Jesus that we are saved and belong to God and His family (a onetime act). Then we start a lifelong growth of faith, becoming more able to love unconditionally. Then we are truly able to bless others with unconditional love. In the following weeks we will look at each characteristic individually.

My Notes

WEEK THIRTY

Love is Patient

Patience is "the capacity, habit, or fact of being patient" or being "steadfast despite opposition, difficulty or adversity."[1]

"Be completely humble and gentle; be patient, bearing with one another in love."

Ephesians 4:2 NIV

---

1. Woolf, Henry Bosley, *Webster's New Collegiate Dictionary*, (G. & C. Merriam Company 1977), 840

Thoughts to Ponder This Week

» Unconditional love requires a humble heart.
» Gentleness leads to patience.
» Patience: a way to win over difficult people.

As with many, patience is a challenge for me. I have grown in that area; however, when I start to feel I have a handle on patience, I face a challenge that shows me I still need growth in that area. One challenge for me is one of my best friends and brother in the Lord. He has a big heart and is always ready to help when you are in need. That being said, we seem to have the ability to push each other's buttons. Even though it is getting easier, I still find myself having to work at being patient with him. Isn't it strange that the people we are closest to can be the very ones that try our patience? I have another friend I feel a great love for, but more than that I have made the decision to love her unconditionally whether I feel it or not. Remember, unconditional love is more than a feeling; it's a decision to love in a way that seeks what is best for the other person. It is a decision to be patient with them whether you feel it or not.

My Notes

WEEK THIRTY-ONE

Love is Kind

"Affectionate, loving; of a sympathetic nature; disposed to be helpful."[2]

"Be kind and compassionate to one another, forgiving each other, just as in Christ God forgave you."

Ephesians 4:32 NIV

---

2. Woolf, Henry Bosley, *Webster's New Collegiate Dictionary*, (G. & C. Merriam Company 1977), 635

Thoughts to Ponder This Week

» Do you have a kind and affectionate heart?
» Are you sympathetic towards others, and willing to be helpful?
» Are you ready and able to forgive others?

Unconditional love is not easy to maintain; however, it is vital in the Christian's life. We are called by God to love others and to be kind as one aspect of love. Some people are easy to be kind to; others are more of a challenge. However, that fact really doesn't matter; the fact that we are called to be kind to all those around us is what matters. God desires that we be helpful to those in need, and that we be willing to forgive others just like God has forgiven us. Let us pray that God will fill us with His love and show us the way to let kindness flow to others, that He will take away our anger, bitterness, and selfishness and give us a heart of kindness and compassion towards others.

My Notes

WEEK THIRTY-TWO

Love Does Not Envy

"Painful or resentful awareness of an advantage enjoyed by another join with the desire to possess the same advantage."[3]

"For where you have envy and selfish ambition, there you will find disorder and every evil practice."

James 3:16 NIV

---

3. Woolf, Henry Bosley, *Webster's New Collegiate Dictionary*, (G. & C. Merriam Company 1977), 382

Thoughts to Ponder This Week

» Do you desire to have what others have?
» Are you grateful for what you have?
» Ambition is a good trait to have; selfish ambition comes from an envious heart.

Envy leads to selfish ambition that will hurt others to gain what they have for your own. It can be the seeking of possessions or of relationships. Unconditional love, on the other hand, seeks what is best for others and is grateful to see them do well. It is the love that restores relationships and comfort to the hurting. Unconditional love is the key to solving the challenges of life. Where you have unconditional love you will have happiness, contentment, and every good practice.

My Notes

WEEK THIRTY-THREE

Love Does Not Boast

"To puff oneself up in speech, to speak of or assert with excessive pride, to possess and often call attention to (something that is a source of pride)."[4]

"These men are grumblers and faultfinders; they follow their own evil desires; they boast about themselves and flatter others for their own advantage."

Jude 16 NIV

---

4. Woolf, Henry Bosley, *Webster's New Collegiate Dictionary*, (G. & C. Merriam Company 1977), 123

Thoughts to Ponder This Week

- » Do you boast out of low self-esteem?
- » Do you boast out of pride?
- » Unconditional love does not boast.

Sometimes a person will boast or brags about themselves out of low self-esteem, feeling that somehow others are better than they are. Other times a person will boast or blow their own horn out of pride, feeling they are better than others. Either way, it is a selfish means to bring attention to oneself and take it away from others. Boasting comes from a cold, self-seeking heart, whereas love comes from a warm, caring heart. You need love for yourself in order to realize you are neither less worthy than others nor more important than they are. Unconditional love provides the balance needed to be caring and kind to yourself, and at the same time show compassion to others.

My Notes

WEEK THIRTY-FOUR

Love is Not Proud

"Feeling or showing pride as having or displaying excessive self-esteem."[5]

"Live in harmony with one another. Do not be proud, but be willing to associate with people of low position. Do not be conceited."

Romans 12:16 NIV

---

5. Woolf, Henry Bosley, *Webster's New Collegiate Dictionary*, (G. & C. Merriam Company 1977), 928

Thoughts to Ponder This Week

» Do you look down at those who you feel are of inferior quality to you?
» Do you interact with people in an arrogant manner or with respect?
» Consider the unassuming nature of Jesus and the self-importance of the religious leaders.

Excessive self-esteem leads to a prideful attitude towards others. It brings about disrespect and false judgment towards others. A prideful heart has little room for love. On the other hand, a heart filled with love has plenty of room for an abundance of kindness and compassion. May we not be hard-hearted towards those who are suffering, but treat them with love and mercy. Let us have a desire to help those in need. Remember, pride stifles relationships while love builds relationships.

My Notes

WEEK THIRTY-FIVE

Love is Not Rude

"Offensive in manner or action: Discourteous."[6]

"Finally, brothers, whatever is true, whatever is pure, whatever is lovely, whatever is admirable, if anything is excellent or praiseworthy—think about such things."

Philippians 4:8 NIV

---

6. Woolf, Henry Bosley, *Webster's New Collegiate Dictionary*, (G. & C. Merriam Company 1977), 1011

Thoughts to Ponder This Week

» Consider how the above verse fits with the concept of unconditional love.
» Rudeness has no place in a kind heart.
» Reflect on ways you can become kinder and less rude.

Rudeness seems to be a natural aspect of our lives. It comes out our mouths without a thought. It shows up in our actions without a single care. Kindness, on the other hand, is something we must practice with thought and effort to make it a part of our lives. Remember, kindness is an attribute of unconditional love. Unconditional love is more than a feeling we have towards someone. It is also a decision we make to have unconditional love for someone. When we feel like being rude to someone and decide to have unconditional love for them instead, we will be better able to show them kindness. Remember love is kind; it is not rude.

My Notes

WEEK THIRTY-SIX

Love is Not Self-seeking

"The act or practice of selfishly advancing one's own ends. Seeking only to further one's own interests."[7]

Do nothing out of selfish ambition or vain conceit, but in humility consider others better than yourselves. Each of you should look not only to your own interests, but also to the interests of others. Your attitude should be the same as that of Christ Jesus: Who, being in very nature God, did not consider equality with God something to be grasped, but made himself nothing, taking the very nature of a servant, being made in human likeness. And being found in appearance as a man, he humbled himself and became obedient to death – even death on a cross!

Philippians 2:3-8 NIV

---

7. Woolf, Henry Bosley, *Webster's New Collegiate Dictionary*, (G. & C. Merriam Company 1977), 1051

Thoughts to Ponder This Week

» Are your attitudes and actions towards others an outpouring of your desire for your own interests?
» Do you have a desire to help others in need?
» Do you consider your own interests only or do you also consider the interests of others?

When we discuss the concept of unconditional love not being self-seeking, we are not saying you should disregard your own interests or goals. We need to consider our own interests and goals. Remember, working towards our own interests is not the same as being self-seeking. Self-seeking is a selfish attitude that places our own needs or concerns over others. It brings actions for self-gain whether it hurts others or not. Unconditional love calls for a balance between our concerns and the concerns of others. Remember, to be able to love others we must love ourselves. That too requires a balance. May we not be self-seeking, but rather have a healthy balance between concern for self and concern for others. May we maintain a healthy unconditional love for ourselves as well as others.

My Notes

WEEK THIRTY-SEVEN

Love is Not Easily Angered

"My dear brothers, take note of this: Everyone should be quick to listen, slow to speak and slow to become angry, for a man's anger does not bring about the righteous life that God desires."

James 1:19-20 NIV

Thoughts to Ponder This Week

» Do you take time to listen and consider what was said?
» Do you speak from a reaction of what you have seen or heard or do you take time to consider your thoughts before speaking?
» Do you tend to act out of anger or do you tend to be a peace keeper?

If unconditional love is not easily angered, what are some tools we can use to avoid becoming angry? First off, we should be kindhearted towards the person pushing our buttons. We should take time to listen or consider what we have seen. Then we should think about what we should say before we speak. We should try to be a peace keeper if possible. That being said, there are times we need to defend our family, friends, and ourselves. We may even be called on to defend another person we don't know. All those can be examples of unconditional love. So what about the anger. Remember, it said "does not become easily angered." There are times and things to be angry about; the key is know when it is okay to be angry and how to handle it. Unconditional love is not easily angered; however, it does not stand by when someone is hurting another.

My Notes

WEEK THIRTY-EIGHT

Love Does Not Keep Record of Wrongs

"Hatred stirs up dissension, but love covers over all wrongs."

Proverbs 10:12 NIV

"Above all, love each other deeply, because love covers over a multitude of sins. Offer hospitality to one another without grumbling. Each one should use whatever gift he has received to serve others, faithfully administering God's grace in its various forms."

1 Peter 4:8-10 NIV

THOUGHTS TO PONDER THIS WEEK

» Do you keep track of all wrongs done to you, with a bitter heart?
» Do you dismiss wrongs done to you, with a compassionate heart?
» Do you follow God's example and calling not to keep a record of wrongs, through unconditional love?

I remember a story my mom told me about one time when dad went around the house for days irritable and ill-tempered. When she asked him what was wrong, he said, "I don't know I just know I am mad about something." After she confronted him about that, he was finally able to let go and get back to being his happy and friendly self. He was keeping record of a wrong (even though he couldn't even remember what the wrong was) and it was hurting his relationships and making his heart sad. When he let go of the wrong, it gave him a happy, loving heart and helped his relationships. We can choose to hold on to a wrong committed by someone in our lives and have it to throw back at them in the future, which will only hurt the relationship and make us bitter. Or we can choose to forgive them of the wrong and let go of it, which will heal the relationship and give us a loving heart. Remember, God chose to love us and forgive the wrongs committed by those who choose to believe in Him, thus bringing about a healing relationship with Him. We can choose to love those who have wronged us and let the wrong go, thus healing and strengthening the relationship. Remember, choosing unconditional love means choosing not to keep a record of wrongs.

My Notes

WEEK THIRTY-NINE

Love Does Not Delight in Evil

The Greek word used here for evil is αδικια (adikia). It can be defined in English as "(legal) injustice (properly, the quality, by implication, the act); morally, wrongfulness (of character life or act)"[8]

"Trust in the Lord with all your heart and lean not on your own understanding; in all your ways acknowledge him, and he will make your paths straight. Do not be wise in your own eyes; fear the Lord and shun evil."

Proverbs 3:5-7 NIV

---

8. (Copyright © 1994, 2003, 2006 Biblesoft, Inc. and International Bible Translators, Inc.) (Biblesoft's *New Exhaustive Strong's Numbers and Concordance with Expanded Greek-Hebrew Dictionary*)

Thoughts to Ponder This Week

- » Do you fully trust in the Lord, or do you delight in activities that are evil?
- » Do you act based on your own understanding of right and wrong?
- » Do your actions towards others come from a kind and loving heart?

Loving someone is more than a feeling; it is also a choice. If you truly love someone, you don't just treat them properly when you feel like it but rather it is a choice you make whether you feel like it or not. Unconditional love does not delight in evil or wrong actions toward others, but rather seeks to treat them with compassion and integrity. An evil or unrighteous heart seeks to do harm for a moment of gain. Unconditional love seeks righteousness and kindness as a way of life. May the desire to show compassion towards others grow in your heart as you learn how to love God, others, and yourself unconditionally more and more.

My Notes

WEEK FORTY

Love Rejoices in the Truth

The Greek word for truth here is αληθεια (aletheia). "(1) of what has certainty and validity truth (2) of the real state of affairs, especially as divinely disclosed truth (3) of the concept of the gospel message as being absolute truth (2 Thessalonians 2:12) (4) of true-to-fact statements (5) of what is characterized by love of truth *truthfulness*, uprightness, fidelity."[9]

"This is the verdict: Light has come into the world, but men loved darkness instead of light because their deeds were evil. Everyone who does evil hates the light, and will not come into the light for fear that his deeds will be exposed. But whoever lives by the truth comes into the light, so that it may be seen plainly that what he has done has been done through God."
John 3:19-21 NIV

---

9. Friberg Timothy & Barbara, Miller F. Neva, *Analytical Lexicon of the Greek News Testament*, (Trafford Publishing 2005) 42

Thoughts to Ponder This Week

» Do you fear being exposed as treating people thoughtlessly or being mean spirited?
» Do you enjoy doing acts of kindness and compassion for others?
» Do you rejoice in the absolute truth of the gospel message?

If we truly love God, we will rejoice in the truth of His Word. If we truly love ourselves, we will take joy in living according to the truth. If we truly love others, we will delight in treating them based on the truth of unconditional love. The truth of showing unconditional love is that you will treat others with thoughtfulness, providing sympathy for those who are hurting, being kind hearted and having compassion towards others. May we not take pleasure in treating people with an evil objective, but rather truly treating them with excellent motives.

My Notes

WEEK FORTY-ONE

Love Always Protects

"We who are strong ought to bear with the failings of the weak and not to please ourselves. Each of us should please his neighbor for his good, to build him up. Accept one another, then, just as Christ accepted you, in order to bring praise to God."

Romans 15:1-2, 7 NIV

"Brothers, if someone is caught in a sin, you who are spiritual should restore him gently. But watch yourself, or you also may be tempted. Carry each other's burdens, and in this way you will fulfill the law of Christ."

Galatians 6:1-2 NIV

Thoughts to Ponder This Week

» Would you want to do anything that would hurt someone you love, or would you want to protect them from harm?
» Would you want the best for someone you love even if it means you may have to make a sacrifice?
» Do you give someone you love your full support with their concerns?

Those of us who are believers in Jesus Christ are called to love one another. Part of that love and calling is to be willing to protect each other. We are to bear their burdens, and to save them from harm. Unconditional love will guide us to care for someone who is hurting and heal their pain. Granted, there are those relationships that are much closer than others; however, we are called to show compassion and kindness to all. As part of God's family, it's our responsibility to help those in need through love. Remember, when we accept each other and show love to each other, we fulfill the teaching of Jesus and bring praise to God the Father, Son, and Spirit.

My Notes

WEEK FORTY-TWO

Love Always Trusts

The Greek word used here for trust is πιστευο (pisteuo) and is defined by Friberg "(3) as committing something to someone entrust, trust; passive, as having something committed to someone be entrusted with."[10]

"To my dear friend Galius, whom I love in the truth. Dear Friend, you are faithful in what you are doing for the brothers, even though they are strangers to you. They have told the church about your love. You will do well to send them on their way in a manner worthy of God."

3 John 1 & 5-6 NIV

---

10 Friberg Timothy & Barbara, Miller F. Neva, *Analytical Lexicon of the Greek New Testament*, (Trafford Publishing 2005) 314

Thoughts to Ponder This Week

- » Do you love others unconditionally?
- » Are you compassionate?
- » Are you trustworthy?

Trust is a worthwhile quality in a relationship based in unconditional love. Often in relationships today, trust is broken, people are mistreated, and they end in hurt feelings. However, when two people are in a relationship where they truly love each other unconditionally, they will want the best for each other. They will support each other and respect the other. In such a relationship, you can trust they will not betray you or hurt you. You know that they will show you kindness and always be there for you. In that loving relationship, you will prove yourself to be trustworthy. Trust can be hard to come by, but it does come a lot easier when it comes through love.

My Notes

WEEK FORTY-THREE

Love Always Hopes

The Greek word here for hope is ελπιξει (elpizei). Friberg defined it as "(1) in the sense of counting on something expect, await, hope for (2) as relying on a basis of confidence hope in, trust in, confidence in."[11]

"And now these three remain: faith, hope, and love. But the greatest of these is love."

1 Corinthians 13:13 NIV

---

11. Friberg Timothy & Barbara, Miller F. Neva, *Analytical Lexicon of the Greek New Testament*, (Trafford Publishing 2005) 145

Thoughts to Ponder This Week

- » Do you have faith or trust in others?
- » Do you hope in or have confidence in others?
- » Do you love others?

As we learned in last week's devotion, unconditional love is the basis trust is built on in a relationship. This week we will see that unconditional love is also the basis on which we can have hope or confidence in another. When we truly love someone unconditionally, we will want the best for them. We will not want to hurt them or do anything that would cause them harm. We will support them in their endeavors and give them our protection. We will treat them with kindness and compassion. We will not keep track of wrongs they have done to us or ways they have hurt us, but rather show them forgiveness with a loving heart. These are the kind of loving actions that build hope or confidence in a relationship. For those of us who belong to God's family, the day will come when faith, hope, and love will be perfected in our new lives without sin. However, for now we must work, through the Holy Spirit, at growing in love, thus being further able to bless others with hope.

My Notes

WEEK FORTY-FOUR

Love Always Perseveres

The Greek word here for perseveres is υπομενει (upomenei). Friberg's definition is "(1) with εν and the dative of place remain behind, stay (when others depart) (2) as refusing to flee hold out, stand one's ground, endure (3) with the accusative of the thing be patient under, suffer, endure, put up with (4) absolutely endure, continue firm, persevere."[12]

"We ought always to thank God for you, brothers, and rightly so, because your faith is growing more and more, and the love every one of you has for each other is increasing. Therefore, among God's churches we boast about your perseverance and faith in all the persecutions and trials you are enduring."
2 Thessalonians 1:3-4 NIV

---

12   Friberg Timothy & Barbara, Miller F. Neva, *Analytical Lexicon of the Greek New Testament*, (Trafford Publishing 2005) 392

Thoughts to Ponder This Week

» Is your faith in God growing more and more?
» Is the love you have for each other growing deeper as you spend time together?
» Are you able to stand strong with each other through trials and temptations?

This week we are looking at love within our church family and how through that love we are able to persevere. When we truly have unconditional love for each other we will care for each other. We will rejoice over the good times together and support each other through the challenging times. Through love, we will stand strong with those who are facing hardships or who are hurting. Because of God's love for us and ours for Him and our love for each other, we will be able to endure struggles together. Life can be hard, but it goes much better when we know we have others in our lives that will stand along with us and will help us with our needs. In our culture we take great store in being independent; however, we truly need others who love us and support us in order to be able to endure the challenges of life.

My Notes

WEEK FORTY-FIVE

John 13:34-35

"A new command I give you: Love one another. As I have loved you, so you must love one another. By this all men will know that you are my disciples, if you love one another."

John 13:34-35 NIV

"Let me give you a new command: Love one another. In the same way I loved you, you love one another. This is how everyone will recognize that you are my disciples – when they see the love you have for each other."

John 13:34-35 MSG

Thoughts to Ponder This Week

» How important is it to Jesus that we love each other?
» What are some examples of how Jesus showed His love to us?
» Based on your love for others, would you be recognized as a believer in Jesus?

In these two verses, Jesus tells His disciples three times to love each other. The first time He stated it as a new command. Then He told them to love each other like He loved them. Finally, Jesus told them that they would be recognized as His followers by their love for each other. So it is important to God that we love each other unconditionally. If we are to love each other the same way Jesus did, we must ask how Jesus showed His love towards us. Well, Jesus showed His compassion by addressing the needs of people. He cared for those who were hurting. He showed His disciples what it meant to be a servant to each other by washing their feet. Most of all, Jesus put His love into action by dying a humble death on a cross so we could be restored back into a true, loving relationship with God. So if we truly love each other as Jesus loves us, we should have a servant's heart towards each other. We should show compassion to those who are hurting. We should help those in need and be kind to those who are struggling. Like Jesus, we should be willing to give up our lives for others. Finally, the way we love each other is how we will be recognized as true, loving Christians.

My Notes

WEEK FORTY-SIX

1 John 3:16-18

"This is how we know what love is: Jesus Christ laid down his life for us. And we ought to lay down our lives for our brothers. If anyone has material possessions and sees his brother in need but has no pity, how can the love of God be in him? Dear children, let us not love with words or tongue but with actions and in truth."

1 John 3:16-18 NIV

Thoughts to Ponder This Week

> » Do you show your love with words only or also through your actions?
> » Do you have a God-given desire to help people who are struggling?
> » Do you truly love unconditionally?

James said "Show me your faith without deeds, and I will show you my faith by what I do" (James 2:18B NIV). John wrote in his first letter not to love by words, but by our actions in truth. I believe these two statements go hand in hand. If we truly have faith in God and love each other, then we will show it by our actions and not just with our words. God saved Claudia Christian's life from Alcohol Use Disorder and gave her a real desire to help others who are struggling with AUD, and for over a decade she has saved people's lives through a science-based treatment known as the Sinclair Method. God has given me a desire to help people with Alcohol Use Disorder by supporting Claudia's efforts through her non-profit and spreading the word about TSM.

God has led me to help people in small ways as well. One time I saw a person who needed help getting gas for his car. I remember on the way to the gas station he asked me why I was helping him. I said because he was in need. He couldn't believe someone would take the time to help a stranger. What are some ways, big or small, God has given you a desire to help others? If you truly have faith in God and love others, He will give you the desire to help others. All you need to do is listen to His quiet voice and respond to it.

My Notes

WEEK FORTY-SEVEN

Colossians 3:12-14

"Therefore, as God's chosen people, holy and dearly loved, clothe yourselves with compassion, kindness, humility, gentleness and patience. Bear with each other and forgive whatever grievances you may have against one another. Forgive as the Lord forgave you. And over all these virtues put on love, which binds them all together in perfect unity."

Colossians 3:12-14 NIV

Thoughts to Ponder This Week

- » You gain nothing by acts of kindness without love.
- » Have you tried to live a virtuous life without love?
- » Love is the glue that holds the acts of kindness together.

Our actions prove our love, but actions without love prove nothing. For our acts of kindness and gentleness to be worthwhile, they need to be done with love. It is love that provides patience and humility in our lives. Love gives us the ability to truly forgive others. As brothers and sisters in God's family, it is love that holds us together. It is love that keeps us in unity, being able to patiently let one another grow in our faith and become more Christlike. When you find it hard to love and forgive someone (and you will, as we all do), remember God loves you and forgave you. It was Jesus' loving death on a cross that saved your life. We will struggle through this life to be a loving, compassionate person, but with the influence of the Holy Spirit we will be able to struggle less and grow into a more loving and virtuous person.

My Notes

WEEK FORTY-EIGHT

Romans 12:9-13

"Love must be sincere. Hate what is evil; cling to what is good. Be devoted to one another in brotherly love. Honor one another above yourselves. Never be lacking in zeal, but keep your spiritual fervor, serving the Lord. Be joyful in hope, patient in affection, faithful in prayer. Share with God's people who are in need. Practice hospitality."

Romans 12:9-13 NIV

Thoughts to Ponder This Week

- » Self-centered love is a self-seeking, dishonest love.
- » Unconditional love is sincere, seeking the best for others.
- » A person with God's love gladly shares with those in need.

We are called to a sincere love for our brothers and sisters in the Lord. For those of us who are under God's saving love, we ought to take joy in the hope or confidence we have through the grace and mercy of Jesus. Because of that love and hope we have, we are called to be patient with one another, faithfully praying for others with affection. God has brought a friend into my life whom I love like a sister, and it is my honor to pray for her daily. She has been a great encouragement to me in growing my faith. With the challenges of life, we need people in our lives we can depend on and we should show sincere love towards others, proving ourselves trustworthy.

My Notes

WEEK FORTY-NINE

Romans 13:8-10

Let no debt remain outstanding, except the continuing debt to love one another, for he who loves his fellowman has fulfilled the law. The commandments, "o not commit adultery," "Do not murder," "Do not steal," "Do not covet," and whatever other commandment there may be, are summed up in this one rule: "Love your neighbor as yourself." Love does no harm to its neighbor. Therefore love is the fulfillment of the law.

Romans 13:8-10 NIV

Thoughts to Ponder This Week

» Do you practice acts of kindness and honesty towards others out of religious duty or out of unconditional love?
» Do you practice acts of compassion and concern for others out of social justice or out of unconditional love?
» Do you give to those in need for self-seeking reasons or through a sincere unconditional love?

As we learned through our time in the "Love Chapter," 1 Corinthians 13, love does not bring harm to others. We also learned it is nearly impossible to practice a godly lifestyle without having a truly sincere unconditional love. We can try to mandate fair treatment of others or try to follow religious law, but without love we will fall short. It is only through love that we can consistently treat others with goodness and not do harm to them. Through our sin nature we are self-seeking, bringing harm to others for self-gain or gratification. It is only through God's love flowing through us that we can truly love others, without fail, all the time, without any selfish desires. May we love God fully, love ourselves, and love those around us, thus making the world a better place.

My Notes

WEEK FIFTY

Ephesians 5:25-28

Husbands, love your wives, just as Christ loved the church and gave himself up for her to make her holy, cleaning her by washing with water through the word, and to present her to himself as a radiant church, without stain or wrinkle or any other blemish, but holy and blameless. In this same way, husbands ought to love their wives as their own bodies. He who loves his wife loves himself.

Ephesians 5:25-28 NIV

Thoughts to Ponder This Week

» Is this passage just for husbands?
» What is there here for the ladies and single men reading this book?
» What can we all learn about loving others?

Yes, this passage is written to husbands, and we will first look at that aspect and then we will look further as we see how it can speak to all of us and show an aspect of love for all Christians. Remember, in that day women had very few rights, and many times wives were treated badly. The idea that husbands are to love their wives in the same way that Christ loved His church was a revolutionary idea. Yet here we are taught that husbands are to love their wives and treat them as pure, holy ladies. To love them like Christ loves us is to want the best for them. To support them in becoming the persons God intended them to be, to be willing to protect their wives even with their own lives. He who truly loves his wife shows his love for himself.

How does this passage speak to the rest of us? I am glad you asked. We should endeavor to become more like Christ, and the way we love others should be a reflection of that. The friend I talked about in week forty-eight is one whom I have endeavored to love as Christ does, as I have with many of my friends. Our friendship is one that encourages each other to grow in faith and be the people God wants us to be. Christlike love should seek the best for others.

My Notes

WEEK FIFTY-ONE

Galatians 5:4-6

You who are trying to be justified by law have been alienated from Christ; you have fallen away from grace. But by faith we eagerly await through the Spirit the righteousness for which we hope. For in Christ Jesus neither circumcision nor uncircumcision has any value. The only thing that counts is faith expressing itself through love.

Galatians 5:4-6 NIV

Thoughts to Ponder This Week

- » Do you live your life by following a bunch of religious rules?
- » Do you have a true faith in Jesus?
- » Do you express that faith in love?

Unfortunately, there are a lot of people who base their hope on following religious rules, going to church, and good acts. None of that has any value for salvation. Our hope or confidence for salvation comes only through faith in Jesus and that faith being expressed in love. Unconditional love is an outpouring of our faith. Good deeds motivated by unconditional love gives proof that we belong to God's family. It shows we are His sons &and daughters through the grace and love of Jesus granted to those who believe. As we become more like Christ, we are better able to bless others through unconditional love. Remember, faith is expressed through our actions, and unconditional love is also expressed though our actions. However, actions without faith and love gain us nothing.

My Notes

WEEK FIFTY-TWO

1 Corinthians 13:13

"And now these three remain: faith, hope, and love. But the greatest of these is love."

1 Corinthians 13:13 NIV

Thoughts to Ponder This Week

» Do you belong to God's family through faith?
» Do you have hope in the knowledge that God loves you and desires a relationship with you?
» Is unconditional love filling your heart as you grow in faith?

In this life we can grow in faith, have a more secure hope and deeper unconditional love. However ,we will always do battle with our selfish sin nature. Our faith, hope, and love may never be expressed perfectly in this life, but we can become more able to love as our faith grows. For those of us who believe in Jesus, our love can and will become deeper. As our love grows deeper for others, we are better able to trust. Remember, love has no desire to harm others, but to seek goodness for them. Love gives us kindness and compassion without seeking self-gain. Unconditional love may not be perfect in this life, but it can come mighty close. The great news is that in life eternal we will be renewed back into a perfect relationship with God and each other. We will no longer deal with the sin nature. We will have a true hope or confidence through a faith without apprehension. We will have a perfect, unconditional love for God, ourselves, and each other. May your love be proven through your actions.

My Notes

Author's Final Thought

It is my hope that over the last fifty-two weeks you were able to spend time with the Most Holy God reflecting on unconditional love. Hopefully you were able to gain a deeper love for God the Father, Son, and Spirit, and through Him compassion for those around you. May you be a blessing to your family, friends, and neighbors, and may God bless you.

Keep the Faith,

Thomas Howell

My Good Friend

The good friend I wrote about in week three is Claudia Christian, a wonderful lady, and her monster with a wicked heart is alcohol. She won her battle with the monster through the Sinclair Method. TSM is a safe, science-based treatment that helps people who struggle with Alcohol Use Disorder, with an eighty percent success rate. Because of her great compassion for people whose lives are being destroyed by AUD, Claudia has founded a nonprofit called *Options Save Lives*, formally *C Three Foundation*, and is its CEO. Through her efforts, many people have been saved from AUD with the Sinclair Method.

God saved Claudia's life and gave her a desire to help others. She has been a blessing for many people. Claudia shows her love for God and for others through her actions. When I think of Claudia this verse comes to mind: "Show me your faith without deeds, and I will show you my faith by what I do" (James 2:18B NIV). Will you consider being a blessing to Claudia by joining the *Options Save Lives* HERO team (monthly donors)? You can do it on their web site or by scanning the QR code on the next page.

Thomas Howell

Options Save Lives

Helping

Empower

Realistic

Outcomes